QUOTES ON LEADERSHIP

To Inspire You

350 Quotations on Character, Integrity, Vision, Positive attitude, Self-discipline, Priority and Humility

BELISIER CHERY

For permissions request or inquiries, please contact: belisierchery@gmail.com

Cover design and interior design by David Revolte

Published by Belisier Chery

ISBN: 9798862066746
Imprint: Independently published

First Edition: September 2023

DEDICATION

Dedication to my Dad, Dieufort Chery, who taught me the value of taking responsibility and inspired in me a deep love for the Lord.

To my Mom, Marie Therese Chery, my steadfast rock, a woman of unwavering faith who continually intercedes for me before the Lord.

To my pastor, Dr. Kelly Baldé, who ignited my passion for reading and applying the word of God in my life, and encouraged me to walk by faith, not by sight.

To my siblings, Melchisedec Chery and Marie-Carmelle, for their significant roles in my life.

To my friend and mentor, Joey Jenkins, who gifted me leadership books and continuously encouraged me to pursue my dreams.

To my friend and business partner, David Revolte, whose unwavering support fuels my endeavors.

To my friend, Niti Sarran, who imparted invaluable knowledge about digital marketing.

Above all, to my Lord Jesus Christ, who provides me with strength and wisdom to chase my dreams, guides me through challenging times, and safeguards my life.

QUOTES ON LEADERSHIP TO INSPIRE YOU

CONTENTS

DEDICATION ii

Introduction 1

Character 3

Integrity 18

Vision 49

Commitment 64

Self-discipline 81

Priority 97

Humility 111

ADDITIONAL LEADERSHIP QUOTES 126

CONCLUSION 147

BILIOGRAPHY 148

About the Author 148

QUOTES ON LEADERSHIP TO INSPIRE YOU

Introduction

Leadership is not merely a position one holds; it is an internal journey. True leadership begins within oneself. Often, leadership is mistaken as obtaining a title, rather than amassing followers. It's important to understand that leadership doesn't necessitate a position, but rather a conscious decision to adopt a leadership mindset and cultivate specific qualities that enable the influence of others. These qualities are the foundation of all exceptional leaders.

John C. Maxwell delves into these essential qualities in his book "21 Indispensable Qualities of a Leader," emphasizing their critical role in effective leadership. Moreover, exploring Maxwell's work in "Developing the Leader within You" reveals that leadership is not just an external position, but also an internal development process. This journey involves nurturing attributes such as character, vision, integrity, positive attitude, self-discipline, and more.

In this compilation, I present a collection of insightful statements on integrity, character, self-discipline, vision, priority, positive attitude and humility. These quotes are drawn from the wealth books and articles I have read and consulted. My aim is to share these thought-provoking statements that can profoundly impact your life.

I've meticulously gathered 350 statements on the aforementioned topics. I believe these quotes will serve as a source of inspiration and guidance as you strive to unlock your fullest potential. However, not all the authors or people I quote completely align with my beliefs and values. I only share their sayings about leadership qualities that can make a difference in your life.

Thank you for investing your time in reading this compilation. I trust that these statements will empower you on your journey towards becoming the best version of yourself.

Belisier Chery

Character

Character is the foundation of true leadership (influence). As John C. Maxwell teaches, leadership isn't about titles or positions—it's about one life influencing another. While skills and knowledge are important, it is a leader's character—rooted in integrity, values, and consistency— that earns lasting trust. People follow character before they follow a vision. When leaders operate with honesty, humility, and genuine care for others, they build a culture of loyalty and respect. Character also becomes most evident in times of pressure and uncertainty.

The real test of leadership is not how someone leads when things are easy, but how they respond when the stakes are high. Leaders of character choose what is right over what is easy, and in doing so, they model the kind of ethical courage that inspires others. Maxwell often reminds us that leadership develops daily, not in a day— meaning that character must be cultivated intentionally and consistently. Those who lead by example, embrace personal growth, and serve others with authenticity are the ones who leave a lasting impact. Ultimately, it's not merely what a leader does that defines their influence— it's who they are.

"

Character makes trust possible, and trust is the foundation
of leadership.
-John C. Maxwell

"

Leadership without character is unthinkable or should be.
-Warren Bennis

"

True leadership is determined by character.
-Myles Munroe

"

Character will reflect itself in consistent behavior, while
poor character will seek to hide behind deceptive words
and actions.

-Myles Munroe

"

Your success stops where your character stops, you will never rise above the limitation of your character.
-John C. Maxwell

"

Absolute power doesn't corrupt, but rather, reveals character.
-Orrin Woodward

"

A true athlete should have character, not a character.
-John Wooden

"

Money is either a good or bad influence, according to the character of the person who possesses it.
-Napoleon Hill

"

A man of character will make himself worthy of any position he is given.
-Mahatma Gandhi

"

Your character defines who you are by the actions you take.
-Catherine Pulsifer

"

Character is the moral strength to do the right thing even when it costs more than you want to pay.
-Michael Josephson

"

Primary Greatness is on the inside. It's about character.
-Stephen Covey

"

Any fool can criticize, condemn and complain—and most fools do. But it takes character and self-control to be understanding and forgiving.
-Dale Carnegie

"

Leadership is not a position. It is a combination of something you are (Character) and something you do (competence).
-Ken Melrose

"

Character, not circumstances, make the man.
-Booker T.Washington

"

People will follow you when you build the character to follow through.
-Orrin Woodward

"

Integrity is the glue that holds our way of life together.
We must constantly strive to keep our integrity intact.
"When wealth is lost, nothing is lost; when health is lost,
something is lost; when character is lost, all is lost.
-Billy Graham

"

Sow an action and reap a habit: sow a habit and reap a
character; sow a character and reap a destiny.
-Napoleon Hill

"

Nearly all men can stand adversity, but if you want to test
a man's character, give him power.
-Abraham Lincoln

"

If you don't demonstrate leadership character, your skills,
and results will be discounted, if not dismissed.
-Mark Killer

"

Character cannot be developed in ease and quiet. Only through experience of trial and suffering can the soul be strengthened, ambition inspired, and success achieved.
-Hellen Keller

"

Good character is more to be praised than outstanding talent. Most talents are to some extent, a gift. Good character, by contrast, is not given to us. We have built it, piece by piece– by thought, choice, courage, and determination.
-H Jackson Brown Jr

"

People are interested in talent. God is impressed by character.
-Rick Warren

"

People of character do the right thing even if no one else does, not because they think it will change the world but because they refuse to be changed by the world.

-Michael Josephson

"

Conduct is the best proof of character.

-Unknown

"

Bad things happen; how I respond to them defines my character and the quality of my life. I can choose to sit in perpetual sadness…or I can choose to rise from the pain and treasure the most precious gift I have-life itself.

-Walter Anderson

"

When the character of a man is not clear to you, look at his friends.

-Japanese Proverb

"

Character is the real foundation of all worthwhile success.
-John Hays Hammond

"

Be more concerned with your character than your reputation, because your character is what you really are, while your reputation is merely what others think you are.
-John Wooden

"

You express the truth of your character with the choice of your actions.
-Steve Maraboli

"

No change of circumstances can repair a defect of character.
-Ralph Waldo Emerson

"

Our Character is defined by what we do when we think
no one is looking.
-Anonymous

"

Intelligence plus character is the goal of true education.
-Martin Luther King, Jr

"

The measure of a man's real character is what he would
do if he knew he would never be found out.
-Thomas B. Macaulay

"

Real richness is when you are so expensive that no one
can buy your character.
-Anonymous

"

There's something wrong with your character if opportunity controls your loyalty.

-Sean Simons

"

People of good intentions make promises. People of good character keep them.

-Anonymous

"

It takes real character to do what's right when no one else is doing it.

Anonymous

"

Good character is not formed in a week or a month. It is created little by little, day by day. Protracted and patient effort is needed to develop good character.

-Heraclitus

"

Habits change into character.

-Ovid

"

Knowledge will give you power, but character respect.

-Bruce Lee

"

No one is born with good character; it's not a hereditary trait. And it isn't determined by a single noble act. Character is established by conscientious adherence to moral values, not by lofty rhetoric or good intentions.

-Michael Josephson

"

Character is revealed when pressure is applied.

-Unknown

"

Every problem is a character–Building opportunity.
-Rick Warren

"

Parents can only give their children good advice or put them on the right path, but the final form of a person's character lies in their own hands.
-Anne Frank

"

Character is destiny.
-Heraclitus

"

Leadership is character in action.
-James Hunter

"

Character building begins in our infancy and continues
until death.
-Eleanor Roosevelt

"

If you have no character to lose, people will have no faith
in you.
-Mahatma Gandhi

"

Men of genius are admired, men of wealth are envied,
and men of power are feared: but only men of character
are trusted.
-Alfred Adler

Integrity

Integrity is the cornerstone of authentic leadership. It is more than just honesty—it is a deep, unwavering commitment to moral and ethical principles, even when faced with pressure, temptation, or personal sacrifice. Leaders who embody integrity earn the trust and respect of those they serve, not simply through their words, but through consistent actions that align with their values. This consistency creates a foundation of credibility, enabling open dialogue, collaboration, and innovation to flourish.

Integrity also acts as a guiding compass in moments of tough decision-making, helping leaders navigate ethical dilemmas with clarity and conviction. In doing so, they model the kind of principled leadership that inspires others to follow suit. The presence of integrity fosters a culture of accountability and fairness, while its absence can quickly erode trust, damage relationships, and compromise the health of an entire organization. Ultimately, integrity is not just a leadership trait —it is a leadership necessity. It defines who a leader is, shapes how they lead, and determines the legacy they leave behind.

"

With integrity, you have nothing to fear, since you have nothing to hide. With integrity, you will do the right thing, so you will have no guilt.

-Zig Ziglar

"

Integrity is not something you show others. It is how you behave behind their back.

-Anonymous

"

Integrity is choosing courage over comfort; choosing what is right over what is fun, fast or easy; and choosing to practice our values rather than simply professing them.

-Brene Brown

"

Characterize people by their actions and you will never be fooled by their words.

–Anonymous

"

Love and truth form a good leader; sound leadership is founded on loving integrity.

-Prov. 20:28

"

You can preach a better sermon with your life than with your lips.

-Oliver Goldsmith

"

Integrity is the essence of everything successful.

-R. Buckminster Fuller

"

Integrity without knowledge is weak and useless, and knowledge without integrity is dangerous and dreadful.

-Samuel Johnson

"

Image is what people think we are. Integrity is what we really are.
-John C. Maxwell

"

Real integrity is doing the right thing, knowing that nobody's going to know whether you did it or not.
-Oprah Winfrey

"

Moral authority comes from following universal and timeless principles like honesty, integrity, and treating people with respect.
-Stephen Covey

"

No matter how educated, talented, rich, or cool you believe you are, how you treat people tells all. Integrity is everything.

-Anonymous

"

Integrity is doing the right thing, even when no one is watching.

-C.S. Lewis

"

Integrity is a concept of consistency of actions, values, methods, measures and principles, expectations, and outcomes. It can be regarded as the opposite of hypocrisy.

-Anonymous

"

Integrity is making sure that the things you say and the things you do are in alignment.
-Katrina Mayer

"

Whoever is careless with the truth in small matters cannot be trusted with important matters.
-Albert Einstein

"

The integrity of men is to be measured by their conduct, not by their professions.
-Junius

"

A life lived with integrity — even if it lacks the trappings of fame and fortune is a shining star in whose light others may follow in the years to come.
-Denis Waitley

"

Integrity is the heart of character, don't lose it.
-Anonymous

"

I respect those who tell the truth no matter how hard it is.
Integrity is everything.
-Anonymous

"

If you don't have integrity, you have nothing. You can't
buy it. You can have all the money in the world, but if
you are not a moral and ethical person, you really have
nothing. -Henry Kravis

"

Be the same person privately, publicly, and personally. -
Anonymous

"

Although followers will forgive a leader much, they will never forgive a lack of integrity.

-Peter Drucker

"

Integrity is the ability to accept ones past choices and actions and go forth and act in accordance with ones deepest values from within.

-Lynne Namka

"

Have the courage to say no. Have the courage to face the truth. Do the right thing because it is right. These are the magic keys to living your life with integrity.

-W. Clement Stone

"

A person of integrity is one who has established a system of values against which all of life is judged.

-V. Gilbert Beers

"

There are two kinds of people: Those who do the work
and those who take the credit. Try to be in the first group;
there is less competition there.
-Indira Gandhi

"

The time is always right to do what is right.
-Martin Luther King Jr.

"

Honest and integrity are absolutely essential for success
in life and anyone can develop both qualities.–
Anonymous

"

There can be no friendship without confidence and no
confidence without integrity.
-Samuel Johnson

"

Integrity is when we say the same things publicly that we say privately.
-Simon Sinek

"

People of integrity expect to be believed. They also know time will prove them right and are willing to wait.-Ann Landers

"

Everyone thinks of changing the world, but no one thinks of changing himself.
-Count Leo Tolstoy

"

When you are able to maintain your own highest

standards of integrity—regardless of what others may do—

you are destined for greatness.

-Napoleon Hill

"

Integrity is telling myself the truth. And honesty is telling the truth to other people.

-Spencer Johnson

"

Listen with curiosity. Speak with honesty. Act with integrity.

-Roy T. Bennett

"

Courage combined with integrity is the foundation of character.

-Brian Tracy

"

Integrity is choosing your thoughts and actions based on values rather than personal gain.

-Chris Karcher

"

Integrity means that we are trustworthy and dependable, and our character is above reproach.
-Billy Graham

"

In looking for people to hire, look for three qualities: Integrity, intelligence, and energy. And if they don't have the first, the other two will kill you.
-Warren Buffet

"

Develop your character so that you are a person of integrity.
-Peter Gain

"

If you can maintain your standards and your integrity and you fail, it's ok. It's when you sell out and fail that you feel pretty sick inside.

-Bonnie Hunt

"

The qualities of a great man are vision, integrity, courage, understanding, the power of articulation, and profundity of character.

-Dwight D. Eisenhower

"

Work hard to achieve integrity in your work and your relationships with the people you work with.

-Rebel Wilson

"

Everyone makes mistakes, but only a person with integrity owns up to them.

-Nicole Guillaume

"

Some say if you want success surround yourself with successful people. I say if you want true and lasting success surround yourself with people of integrity.
-Charles F. Glassman

"

Faith that is not evidenced by a life of integrity is not biblical faith at all.
-David Jeremiah

"

Live so that when your children think of fairness, caring, and integrity, they think of you.

-H. Jackson brown

"

In order to be a leader a man must have followers. And to have followers, a man must have their confidence. Hence, the supreme quality for a leader is unquestionably integrity. Without it, no real success is possible, no matter whether it is on a section gang, a football field, in an army, or in an office. If a man's associates find him guilty of being phony, if they find that he lacks forthright integrity, he will fail. His teachings and actions must square with each other. The first great need therefore, is integrity and high purpose.

-Dwight Eisenhower

Positive Attitude

A positive attitude is far more than an admirable trait—it is a powerful expression of inner conviction and clarity of purpose. Effective leadership begins within; it is not defined by status or title, but by a deep awareness of the responsibility to serve, inspire, and develop others. Leaders who consistently approach life and work with a positive mindset do more than uplift spirits—they carry vision. They recognize that challenges are inevitable, but they choose to see obstacles as opportunities for growth rather than limitations.

This mindset fosters emotional intelligence, strengthens morale, and creates an atmosphere of trust, empathy, and collaboration. In times of uncertainty, positive leaders become steady anchors, offering perspective, calm, and direction. Their words bring clarity, and their presence builds confidence.

As Dr. Myles Munroe noted, "Your attitude creates your world and designs your destiny." A leader's mindset does not only shape their own influence—it sets the tone for the entire organization. Through a posture of consistent optimism rooted in purpose, leaders activate potential in others, nurture resilience, and cultivate a culture where growth and excellence can thrive.

"

Keep your thoughts positive because your thoughts become your words. Keep your words positive because your words become your behavior. Keep your behavior positive because your behavior becomes your habits. Keep your habits positive because your habits become your values. Keep your values positive because your values become your destiny.

-Mahatma Gandhi

"

I have found the paradox, that if you love until it hurts, there can be no more hurt, only more love.

-Mother Teresa

"

Optimism is a happiness magnet, if you stay positive, good things and good people will be drawn to you.

-Mary Lou Retton

"

Being defeated is often a temporary condition. Giving up is what makes it permanent.

-Marilyn Vos Savant

"

Be thankful for what you have: you'll end up having more. If you concentrate on what you don't have, you will never, ever have enough.

-Oprah Winfrey

"

If you have a positive attitude and constantly strive to give your best effort, eventually you will overcome your immediate problems and find you are ready for greater challenges.

-Pat Riley

"

There is nothing more powerful as attitude.

-Myles Munroe

"

Teach your children early not to pass the blame or make excuses, but to take responsibility for their actions -Eric Greitens

"

If something is important enough, even if the odds are against you, you should still do it.
-Elon Musk

"

If you don't like something, change it. If you can't change it, change your attitude.
-Maya Angelou

"

If you can dream it, then you can have it. You will get all you want in life if you help enough other people get what they want.
-Zig Ziglar

"

I'm not a product of my circumstances. I am a product of my decisions.
-Stephen Covey

"

If you're not making mistakes, then you're not doing anything. I'm positive that a doer makes mistakes.
-John Wooden

"

You are never too old to set another goal
or dream a new dream.
-C.S Lewis

"

Life is a gift, and it offers us the privilege, opportunity, and responsibility to give Something back by becoming more.
-Tony Robbins

"

The two most important days in your life are the day you are born and the day you find out why.
-Mark Twain

"

Take the attitude of a student, never be too big to ask questions, and never know too much to learn something new.
-Maya Angelou

"

Our attitude towards life determines
life's attitude towards us.
-John Mitchell

"

It's our attitude at the beginning of a difficult task that, more than anything else, will affect
its successful outcome.
-William James

"

The most important thing you'll ever wear is your attitude.

-Jeff Moore

"

When one door of happiness closes, another opens, but often we look so long at the closed door that we do not see the one that has been opened for us.

-Helen Keller

"

A bad attitude is a flat tire, you won't get anywhere until you change it.

-Unknown

"

Attitude is the little thing that makes a big difference.

-Winston Churchill

"

Nurture your mind with great thoughts, for you will never go any higher than you think.
-Benjamin Disraeli

"

A positive attitude can really make dreams come true-It did for me.
-David Bailey

"

Your attitude, not your aptitude, will determine your altitude.
-Zig Ziglar

"

It's most important that you surround yourself with positivity always, and have it in your mind at all times.
-Tyler Perry

"

A positive attitude may not solve every problem but it makes solving problems a more pleasant experience.-
Grant Fairly

"

The lion is king because of attitude.
- Myles Munroe

"

So often, what people say their problem really isn't their problem? Their problem is the attitude which causes them to handle life's obstacles poorly.
-John C. Maxwell

"

Attitude sets the tone, not only for the leader with the attitude, but also for the people following him.
-John C. Maxwell

"

Leadership is practiced not so much in words as in attitude and in actions.
-Harold S. Geneen

"

Your positive action combined with positive thinking results in success.
-Shiv Khera

"

Positive thinking doesn't mean you ignore the reality of the situation. It means you have the optimism, belief and faith to overcome the situation.
-Jon Gordon

"

Positive thinking is more than just a tagline. It changes the way we behave. And I firmly believe that when I am positive, it not only makes me better, but it also makes those around me better.
-Harvey Mackay

"

If you are positive, you'll see opportunities instead of obstacles.
-Confucius

"

If you don't like something, change it. If you can't change it, change your attitude.
-Maya Angelou

"

I don't think of all the misery but of the beauty that still remains.
-Anne Frank

"

To be a great champion you must believe you are the best. If you're not, pretend you are.
-Muhammad Ali

"

Optimism is the faith that leads to achievement; nothing can be done without hope.
-Hellen Keller

"

Having a positive attitude isn't wishy-washy, it's a concrete and intelligent way to view problems, challenges, and obstacles.
-Jeff Moore

"

A positive attitude is a person's passport to a better tomorrow.
-Jeff Keller

"

The only disability in life is a bad attitude.
-Scott Hamilton

"

I'm too busy working on my own grass
to see if yours is greener.
-Unknown

"

Positive thinking will let you do everything better than
negative thinking.
-Zig Ziglar

"

A positive attitude is something everyone can work on,
and everyone can learn how to employ it.
-Captain Jack Sparrow

"

The most important thing you'll
Ever wear is your attitude.
-Jeff Moore

"

Your attitude can take you forward or your attitude can take you down. The choice is always yours.
-Helen Keller

"

Attitudes create your world and design your destiny.
-Myles Munroe

"

True leadership is an attitude that naturally inspires and motivates others, and it comes from internalized discovery about yourself.
-Myles Munroe

Vision

Vision is the heart of effective leadership. It gives direction and purpose, helping people understand where they are going and why it matters. A strong vision does more than set a goal—it inspires people to move forward together toward a future bigger than themselves. When a leader shares this vision clearly and with confidence, it brings people together.

They are more willing to work hard and use their talents because they believe in the leader and the goal. Vision also helps leaders and teams make better decisions by keeping them focused on what really matters, even when challenges come. It helps them see opportunities and adapt to change without fear. More than just a plan, vision touches people's hearts. It draws those who want to be part of something meaningful and encourages them to grow. People don't just follow instructions—they follow leaders who inspire passion.

In short, vision turns good managers into true leaders. It connects people to a purpose, builds strength to keep going, and drives growth for both individuals and organizations. When vision is clear and shared, people move forward because they want to, and that is the true beginning of leadership.

"

Vision is the source and hope of life. The greatest gift ever given to mankind is not the gift of sight, but the gift of vision. Sight is a function of the eyes; vision is a function of the heart. 'Eyes that look are common, but eyes that see are rare.' Nothing noble or noteworthy on earth was ever done without vision.
-Myles Munroe

"

Where there is no vision the people perish.
-Proverbs 29:18

"

Great leaders must have two things: a vision of the world that does not yet exist and the ability to communicate that vision clearly.
-Simon Sinek

"

You must know your dream before you can attract your team.
-John C. Maxwell

"

Vision is the art of seeing what is invisible to others.
-Jonathan Swift

"

Keep your dreams alive. Understand to achieve anything
requires faith and belief in yourself,
Vision, hard work, determination, and dedication.
Remember all things are possible for those who believe.
-Gail Devers

"

The only thing worse than being blind
is having sight but no vision.
-Helen Keller

"

A leader without a vision is like a piano
player without wind.
-Jonathan Michael Bowman

"

All great leaders possess two things: one, they know where they are going, and two, they are able to persuade others to follow.
-John C. Maxwell

"

Leadership is the capacity to translate vision into reality.
-Warren Bennis

"

Vision comes alive when everyone sees where his or her contribution makes a difference."
-Ken Blanchard

"

The best and most beautiful things in the world cannot be seen or even touched-they must be felt with the heart.
-Helen Keller

"

Good business leaders create a vision, articulate the vision, passionately own the vision, and relentlessly drive it to completion.
-Jack Welch

"

Create the highest grandest vision possible for your life, because you become what you believe.
-Oprah Winfrey

"

If you want to reach a goal, you must "see the reaching" in your own mind before you actually arrive at your goal.
-Zig Ziglar

"

Management has a lot to do with answers. Leadership is a function of questions. And the first question for a leader is always: 'Who do we intend to be?' not 'what are we going to do?' but 'who do we intend to be?
-Max Depree

"

You've got to think about big things while you're doing small things, so that all the small things go in the right direction.
-Alvin Toffler

"

When you have a vision it affects your attitude. Your attitude is optimistic rather than pessimistic.
-Charles R. Swindoll

"

Vision is the art of seeing the invisible.
-Jonathan Swift

"

Vision without action is a daydream. Action without vision is a nightmare.
-Japanese Proverb

"

If you are working on something exciting that you really care about, you don't have to be pushed.
The vision pulls you.
-Steve Jobs

"

A leader should be visionary and have more foresight than an employee.
-Jack Ma

"

Vision without action is merely a dream. Action without vision passes the time.
Vision with action can change the world.
–Nelson Mandela

"

A dream is the creative vision for your life in the future. -Denis Waitley

"

Don't expect people to understand your grind when God didn't give them your vision.

-Anonymous

"

Gratitude makes sense of our past, brings peace for today, and creates a vision for tomorrow.

-Melody Beattie

"

Follow those who follow something bigger than themselves - an idea, a belief, a vision, a cause. Run away from those who say we need to follow them.

-Simon Sinek

"

We are limited not by our abilities but by our vision.

-Anonymous

"

Vision is the source of self-discipline.

-Myles Munroe

"

A man without a vision for his future always returns to his past.

-Anonymous

"

A great leader's courage to fulfill his vision comes from passion, not position.

-John Maxwell

"

A movement without vision would be a movement without moral foundation.

-Nelson Mandela

"

One effect of sustained conflict is to narrow our vision of what is possible. Time and time again, conflicts are resolved through shifts that were unimaginable at the start.

-Nelson Mandela

"

Vision is the ability to talk about the future with such clarity it is as if we are talking about the past.

-Simon Sinek

"

Action without vision is only passing time, vision without action is merely a daydreaming, but vision with action can change the world.

-Nelson Mandela

"

Leaders may inspire, but only when the people decide to act does the leader's vision become a movement.

-Simon Sinek

"

Greatness starts with a clear vision of the future.
-Simon Sinek

"

Purpose is when you know and understand what you were born to accomplish. Vision is when you see it in your mind and begin to imagine it.
-Myles Munroe

"

The greatest leaders mobilize others by coalescing people around a shared vision.
-Ken Blanchard

"

Your vision will become clear only when you look into your heart. Who looks outside, and dreams? Who look inside awaken.
-Carl Jung

"

Vision and persistence will get you to the top of the leadership mountain, but only humility
will keep you there.
-Orrin Woodward

"

A leader has the vision and the conviction that a dream can be achieved. He inspires the power and
the energy to get it done.
-Ralph Lauren

"

Good leaders must communicate vision clearly, creatively, and continually. However, the vision does not
come alive until the leader models it.
-John C Maxwell

"

It is unbelievable how powerful you can be when you
have a clear vision.
-Anonymous

"

Leadership is lifting a person's vision to high sights, the raising of a person's performance to the higher standard, the building of personality beyond its normal limitations.
-Peter Drucker

"

Leadership is not about the next election,
it's about the next generation.
-Simon Sinek

"

We all live under the same sky,
but we don't all have the same horizon.
-Konrad Adenauer

"

Followers find the leader and then the vision. Leaders find the vision and then the people.
-John C. Maxwell

"

It takes a leader with vision to see the future leader within the person.

-John C. Maxwell

"

Cherish your visions and dreams as they are the children of your soul: the blueprints of your ultimate achievements.

-Napoleon Hill

Commitment

Commitment is what separates good leaders from great ones. It is more than just showing up or working hard—it is a deep, unwavering pledge to a vision, a mission, and the people being led. This level of dedication builds trust, drives performance, and leaves a lasting impact on both individuals and the organization.

A committed leader leads by example. Their consistency and passion set the tone for the entire team, inspiring others to align their efforts with shared goals. When people see their leader fully invested, they are more likely to give their best in return. This type of leadership creates unity, clarity, and momentum. Commitment also builds credibility. Leaders who follow through on their promises and remain dependable in every circumstance earn the trust of those they lead. In times of uncertainty or adversity, that trust becomes the anchor that holds the team together. It fosters a climate where people feel safe to take risks, innovate, and grow.

During difficult times, commitment is often what makes the difference. While others may retreat in the face of obstacles, committed leaders press forward with focus and resolve. Their steadfastness becomes a source of strength for the entire team, transforming setbacks into opportunities for learning and resilience.

True leadership also involves a commitment to the growth of others. Great leaders invest in the development of their people, offering support, guidance, and opportunities for advancement. This not only enhances individual capabilities but also builds loyalty, motivation, and long-term engagement across the organization.

In the end, commitment is the backbone of impactful leadership. It shapes culture, strengthens relationships, and sustains progress. Leaders who embody commitment create environments where people thrive—and in doing so, they leave behind a legacy marked by growth, achievement, and lasting change.

"

Commitment is what transforms a promise into reality. It is the words that speak badly of your intentions. And the actions which speak louder than the words.
-Abraham Lincoln

"

Interest is setting your alarm the night before. Commitment is not hitting the snooze button the next morning when the alarm goes off.
-Joey Jenkins

"

When you're committed to something, you accept no excuses-only results.
-Ken Blanchard

"

The only limit is your imagination and commitment.
-Tony Robbins

"

Commitment unlocks the doors of imagination, allows
vision, and gives us the right stuff
to turn our dream into reality.

-James Womack

"

If we're really committed to growth, we never stop
discovering new dimensions of self and self-expression

-Oprah Winfrey

"

The greatest things in life all require commitment,
sacrifice, some struggle, and hardship. It's not easy. But
absolutely worth it.

-Robin S. Sharma

"

Your commitments can develop you or destroy you, but
either way, they will define you.

-Rick Warren

"

Encourage your people to be committed to a project
rather than just be involved in it.
-Richard Pratt

"

If you want to take the island, then burn your boats. With
absolute commitment come the insights that create real
victory.
-Tony Robbins

"

Remember that all success is based on long-term
commitment, faith, discipline, attitude, and a few
stepping stones along the way.
-Jim Rohn

"

Integrity is keeping a commitment even after
circumstances have changed.
-David Jeremiah

"

Even though enthusiastic commitment may carry with it the risk of being wrong, still only those who take the chance will ever attain complete creativity. The committed person, win or lose, is the one who finds the real excitement in living.

-Norman Vincent Peale

"

Accountability is the glue that ties commitment to the result.

-Bob Proctor

"

Things never happen by accident. They happen because you have a vision, you have a commitment, and you have a dream.

-Oscar de la Renta

"

Unless commitment is made, there are only promises and hopes…but no plans.

-Peter F. Drucker

"

Dreams come true, but there is a secret. They're realized through the magic of persistence, determination, commitment, passion, practice, focus, and hard work. They happen a step at a time, manifested over years, not weeks.
-Elbert Hubbard

"

Honor your commitments with integrity.
-Les Brown

"

Endeavor to work as hard as possible to attain a new aim with each day that comes by. Don't go to bed until you have achieved something productive.
-Aliko Dangote

"

Taking responsibility is a commitment to own your life, to self-leadership, growth, and freedom.
-Christopher Avery

"

If your organization requires success before commitment,
it will never have either.
-Seth Godin

"

The level of success you achieve will be in direct
proportion to the depth of your commitment.
-Roy T. Bennett

"

When you are surrounded by people who share a
passionate commitment to a common purpose, anything
is possible.
-Howard Schultz

"

Commitment allows you to focus intently on a few highly
important goals and achieve a greater degree of success
than you otherwise would.
-Mark Manson

"

What makes the difference between a great player and just a normal player is dedication, walk, and commitment.
-Thierry Henry

"

Aspire greatly; anything less than a commitment to excellence becomes an acceptance of mediocrity.
-Brian Tracy

"

The how will show up after the commitment to the what.
-Tony Robbins

"

Compassion is not a virtue-it is a commitment. It's not something we have or don't have-it's something we choose to practice.
-Brené Brown

"

Our only hope lies in the power of our love, generosity, tolerance, and understanding and our commitment to making the world a better place for all.

-Muhammad Ali

"

Great changes may not happen right away, but with effort, even the difficult may become easy.

-Bill Blackman

"

Commitment is an act, not a word.

-Jean Paul Sartre

"

Individual commitment to a group effort-that is what makes team work, a company work, a society work, a civilization work.

-Vince Lombardi

"

A relationship requires a lot of work and commitment.
-Greta Scacchi

"

Managers control. Leaders create commitment.
-Jonh Zenger

"

One person with commitment accomplishes more than a thousand with an opinion.
-Orrin Woodward

"

Without commitment you'll never start, but more importantly, without consistency, you'll never finish.
-Denzel Washington

"

There is a difference between interest and commitment. When you're interested in doing something, you do it only when circumstances permit. When you're committed to something, you accept no excuses, only results.
-Art Turock

"

Leaders become great, not because of their power, but for their ability to inspire and elicit commitment, passion, consistent action, and follow-through from others.
-Ty Howard

"

Commitment unlocks the doors of imagination, allows vision, and gives us the right stuff to turn our dream into reality.
-James Womack

"

Unless commitment is made, there are only promises and hopes... but no plans.
-Peter F. Drucker

"

You need to make a commitment, and once you make it, then life will give you some answers.
-Les Brown

"

Things never happen by accident.
They happen because you have a vision, you have a
commitment, and you have a dream.
-Oscar de la Renta

"

Even though enthusiastic commitment may carry with it
the risk of being wrong, still only those who take the
chance will never attain complete creativity. The
committed person, win or lose, is the one who finds the
real excitement in living.
-Norman Vincent Peale

"

Only one who devotes himself to a cause with his whole
strength and soul can be a true master. For this reason,
mastery demands all of a person.
-Albert Einstein

"

The quality of a person's life is in direct proportion to their commitment to excellence, regardless of their chosen field of endeavor.

-Vince Lombardi

"

A leader's job is to develop committed followers. Bad leaders destroy their followers' sense of commitment.

-Dean Smith

"

Leaders will have to give clear and decisive leadership towards a world of tolerance and respect for difference, and an uncompromising commitment to peaceful solutions of conflicts and disputes.

-Nelson Mandela

"

Productivity is never an accident. It is always the results of a commitment to excellence, intelligent planning, and focused effort.

-Paul J. Meyer

"

Personal development is a lifelong commitment to excellence.
-Isaac Mashman

"

If your organization requires success before commitment, it will never have either.
-Seth Godin

"

The biggest commitment you must keep is your commitment to yourself.
-Neale Donald Walsch

Self-discipline

Self-discipline is a foundational trait in effective leadership. It drives consistency, focus, and growth, allowing leaders to pursue their goals with determination while setting a powerful example for others. Leaders who demonstrate self-discipline model high standards in behavior, decision-making, and work ethic—fostering a culture of accountability and trust within their teams.

This trait also enhances time management and prioritization. Disciplined leaders know how to focus on what matters most, ensuring productivity without burnout. In challenging situations, self-discipline helps them remain calm, avoid impulsive decisions, and respond with clarity and purpose—providing much-needed stability to those they lead.

Self-discipline fuels personal growth. Leaders committed to learning and self-improvement remain adaptable and relevant, encouraging their teams to adopt the same mindset. It also plays a key role in goal-setting, helping leaders break down big visions into focused, consistent action.

Most importantly, self-discipline strengthens integrity. Leaders who stay true to their values, even under pressure, earn the lasting respect of their teams. In every way, self-discipline shapes leaders who are trustworthy, resilient, and committed to excellence—laying the foundation for lasting impact and organizational success.

"

Self-discipline begins with the mastery of your thoughts.
If you don't control what you think, you can't control
what you do.
-Napoleon Hill

"

Discipline is the bridge between goals and
accomplishment.
-Jim Rohn

"

Without self-discipline, success is impossible, period.
-Lou Holtz

"

The discipline you enforce today determines the
successes you'll enjoy tomorrow.
-Gary Ryan Blair

"

Discipline is built by consistently performing small acts
of courage.
-Robin Sharma

"

We don't have to be smarter than the rest; we have to be
more disciplined than the rest.
-Warren Buffet

"

Self-command is the main discipline.
-Ralph Waldo

"

It's been said that there are only two pains in life, the pain
of discipline or the pain of regret, and that discipline
weighs ounces while regret weighs tons.
-Tony Robbins

"

A disciplined person follows values stemming from their source-the self.
-Stephen Covey

"

By constant self-discipline and self-control you can develop greatness of character.
-Grenville Kleiser

"

The fact is, discipline is only punishment when imposed on you by someone else. When you discipline yourself, it's not punishment but empowerment.
-Les Brown

"

We must all suffer one of two things: the pain of discipline or the pain of regret and disappointment.
-Jim Rohn

"

Discipline is built by consistently performing small acts of courage.
-Robin Sharma

"

Discipline is giving yourself a command and following it up with action.
-Bob Proctor

"

Self-discipline means establishing authority over one's own habits, routines, and priorities, and not being under their control.
-Oleg Konovalov

"

Respect your efforts, respect yourself. Self-respect leads to self-discipline. When you have both firmly under your belt, that's real power.
-Clint Eastwood

"

Self-discipline is the magic power that makes you
virtually unstoppable.
-Dan Kennedy

"

Self-discipline allows you to obtain better health, better
finances, and a good work ethic, and it allows you to
reach your most difficult goals more efficiently.
-Vishwas Chavan

"

Self-respect is the fruit of discipline; the sense of dignity
grows with the ability to say no to oneself.
-Abraham Joshua Heschel

"

Freedom is not attained through the satisfaction of
desires, but through the suppression of desires.
-Epictetus

"

We do today what they won't, so tomorrow we can accomplish what they can't.
-Dwayne Johnson

"

We all have dreams. But in order to make dreams come into reality, it takes an awful lot of determination, dedication, self-discipline, and effort.
Jesse Owens

"

In reading the lives of great men, I found that the first victory they won was over themselves…self-discipline with all of them came first.
-Harry S Truman

"

Self-discipline is what separates the winners and the losers.
-Thomas Peterffy

"

Self-government won't work without self-discipline.
-Paul Harvey

"

I think self-discipline is something, it's like a muscle. The more you exercise it, the stronger it gets.
-Daniel Goldstein

"

Self-denial and self-discipline, however, will be recognized as the outstanding qualities of a good soldier.
-William Lyon Mackenzie King

"

Discipline equals freedom.
-Jocko Willink

"

We cannot travel without until we first travel within.
-John C. Maxwell

"

The biggest competition you will ever have in this world
is the competition between your disciplined mind and
undisciplined mind.
-James Arthur Ray

"

Great leaders always have self-discipline without
exception.
-John C. Maxwell

"

No person is free who is not master of himself.
-Epictetus

"

If you can get through doing things that you hate to do,
on the other side is greatness.
-David Goggins

"

We must forever conduct our struggle on the high plane of dignity and discipline. We must not allow our creative protest to degenerate into physical violence.
-Martin Luther King, Jr.

"

The more you discipline yourself, the less you will be disciplined by others. Sound Character provides the power with which a person may ride the emergencies of life instead of being overwhelmed by them.
-Napoleon Hill

"

Greatness is not a function of circumstance. Greatness, it turns out, is largely a matter of conscious choice, and discipline.
-Jim Collins

"

The essence of self-discipline is to do the important thing rather than the urgent thing.
-Barry Werner

"

For the Spirit God gave us does not make us timid, but gives us power, love, and self-discipline.
-2 Timothy 1:7

"

No one can make you jealous, angry, vengeful,
Or greedy – unless you let them. Self-discipline is the first rule of all successful leadership.
-Napoleon Hill

"

You will never always be motivated. So you must learn to be disciplined.
-Unknown

"

If you set goals for yourself, and you're like a lot of other people, you probably realize it's not that your goals are physically impossible that's keeping you from achieving them; it's that you lack self-discipline to stick to them. It's physically possible to lose weight. It's physically possible to exercise more.
-Daniel Goldstein

"

The Olympic Games showed us that with self-discipline and dedication, we can be champions.

-Anurag

"

There will have to be rigid and iron discipline before we achieve anything great enduring, and that discipline will not come by mere academic argument or an appeal to reason and logic. Discipline is learned in the school of adversity.

-Mahatma Gandhi

"

Mastering others is strength. Mastering yourself is true power.

-Lao Tzu

"

The only discipline that lasts is self-discipline.

-Bum Phillips

"

Show up, even if you feel tired. That's discipline.

-Uknown

"

Self-respect is the fruit of discipline; the sense of dignity grows with the ability to say no to oneself.

-Abraham Josua Heschel

"

Motivation gets you going, but discipline keeps you growing.

-John C. Maxwell

"

Without self-discipline, success is impossible.

-Lou Holtz

"

Discipline is choosing between what you want now, and what you want most.

-Abraham Lincoln

"

We don't drift into good directions. We discipline and prioritize ourselves there.

-Andy Stanley

Priority

In effective leadership, the ability to prioritize is not just a skill—it's a principle. Great leaders understand that time is limited, and success depends on focusing energy on what matters most. Rather than reacting to every urgent demand, they act based on values and long-term goals, aligning daily actions with a clear vision and purpose.

Leaders who lead with true priorities consistently ask: *What is the highest and best use of my time right now?* They distinguish between the urgent and the important, giving attention to tasks that drive meaningful outcomes instead of simply managing crises. This intentionality not only enhances personal productivity but also sets a powerful example for others to follow.

Prioritization reduces overwhelm by bringing clarity. In high-pressure situations, leaders who know their priorities stay calm and centered. Their focus reassures the team, builds trust, and enables more thoughtful decision-making. By identifying key objectives, they foster a culture where everyone works with direction and shared purpose.

Strategic prioritization also fuels long-term growth. Leaders who habitually evaluate what truly matters are better equipped to seize opportunities, allocate resources wisely, and guide their organizations through change with confidence. Ultimately, prioritizing isn't just about time management—it's about life leadership. When leaders put first things first, they empower their teams, stay aligned with their values, and move consistently toward lasting success.

"

Action expresses priorities.
-Mahatma Gandhi

"

If it's a priority you'll find a way. If it isn't, you'll find an excuse.
-Jim Rohn

"

In a way, I have simplified my life by setting priorities.
-Karen Duffy

"

Nobody is too busy, it's just a matter of priorities.
-Unknown

"

In all planning, you make a list and you set priorities.
-Alan Lakein

"

He only seeks one thing, and but one may hope to achieve it before life is done. But he who seeks all things wherever he goes must reap around him in whatever he sows a harvest of barren regret.
-William H. Hinson

"

You don't get time. You created time.
-Sanhita Baruah

"

To change your life, you need to change your priorities.
-Mark Twain

"

Most of us spend too much time on what is urgent and not enough time on what is important.
-Stephen Covey

"

The first step to success is knowing your priorities.
-Aspesh

"

Focus on your priorities before your priorities lose focus
on you.
-Sarah Leigh

"

The most important thing in life is knowing the most
important things in life.
-Andy Stanley

"

The key is not to prioritize what's on your schedule but to
schedule your priorities.
-Stephen Covey

"

The main thing is to keep the main thing the main thing.
-Stephen Covey

"

When you have too many top priorities, you effectively have no top priorities.
-Stephen Covey

"

If you chase two rabbits, you will not catch either one.
-Russian Proverb

"

You always have time for things you put first.
-Anonymous

"

When you know what's most important to you, making a decision is quite simple.
-Tony Robbins

"

One-half of knowing what you want is knowing what you must give up before you get it.
-Sidney Howard

"

There is never enough time to do everything, but there is always enough time to do the most important thing.
-Brian Tracy

"

You will never find time for anything. If you want time, you must make it.
-Charles Buxton

"

If you continually ask yourself, "what's important now?" then you won't waste time on the trivial.
-Lou Holtz

"

Learn how to separate the majors and the minors. A lot of people don't do well simply because they major in minor things.
-Jim Rohn

"

Lack of time is actually lack of priorities.
-Timothy Ferris

"

Our life is the sum total of all the decisions we make every day, and our priorities determine those decisions.
-Myles Munroe

"

If your activities don't match your priorities, you are wasting your life.
-Rick Warren

"

Living in light of eternity changes your priorities.
-Rick warren

"

You owe it to yourself to make your creative development a top priority.
-Nita Leland

"

You always have time for the things you put first.
-Anonymous

"

People think focus means saying yes to the thing you've got to focus on. But that's not what it means at all. It means saying no to the hundred other good ideas that there are. You have to pick carefully.
-Steve Jobs

"

Life is short. Focus on what really matters most; you should change your priorities overtime.
-Roy T. Bennett

"

Set aside time to plan how you will spend your time. Think about what's most important. Then do those things first.
-Frank Bettger

"

There's nothing like a good night's sleep to remember
what your priorities are.
-Amy Reed

"

Don't be a time manager, be a priority manager. Cut your
major goals into bite-sized pieces.
Each small priority or requirement on the way to ultimate
goal become a mini goal in itself.
-Denis Waitley

"

What seems so necessary today may not even be
desirable tomorrow.
-Martin Luther King

"

Do first things first, and second things not at all.
-Peter Drucker

"

Whatever keeps you from reaching your goals today had better be important - it's costing you a day of your life!
-Nido R. Qubein

"

Make yourself a priority. Fill yourself up so that you can give more to others.
-Oprah Winfrey

"

Lack of direction, not lack of time is the problem. We all have twenty-four-hour days.
-Zig Ziglar

"

Good things happen not by managing time but by prioritizing attention.
-Richie Norton

"

Productivity refers to both the action and the result of a process that centers on assessing one's priorities and then acting on them.
-Melissa Steginus

"

Decide what you want, and decide what you are willing to exchange for it.
Establish your priorities and go to work.
-H. L. Hunt

"

. Without ethics, man has no future. This is to say, mankind without them cannot be itself. Ethics determine choices and actions and suggest difficult priorities
-John Berger

"

Having priorities is essential.
So is having them in the right order.
-Michael Hyatt

"

You define what is important to you by what you dedicate your time to.

-Unknown

"

Never make someone a priority when all you are to them is an option.

-Maya Angelou

"

Be ambitious. Get things done. Keep your priorities straight, your mind right and your head up.

-Unknown

"

Think of your priorities, not in terms of what activities you do, but when you do them. Timing is everything.

-Dan Millman

"

Determine your priorities and focus on them.

-Eileen McDargh

Humility

True humility in leadership is not weakness—it's strength grounded in self-awareness and integrity. As C.S. Lewis wisely noted, humility isn't thinking less of yourself, but thinking of yourself less. Leaders who practice humility shift the focus from personal glory to shared purpose, creating space for others to thrive.

Humble leaders recognize their limitations and remain open to learning from those around them. They listen more than they speak, value diverse perspectives, and foster a culture where every voice matters. This openness not only fuels innovation but builds deep trust within the team.

Rather than seek the spotlight, humble leaders celebrate collective success and give credit where it's due. They lead with gratitude, acknowledging the efforts of others and inspiring loyalty through appreciation. In moments of failure, they take responsibility. In moments of conflict, they seek resolution without ego.

By leading with quiet strength and authenticity, they model the kind of character that inspires. Humility, when lived out, cultivates trust, encourages growth, and builds teams that are grounded in mutual respect and purpose—reflecting the enduring truth that great leadership begins not with pride, but with grace.

"

To be a leader means to have humility, to have respect and serve the people that we are leading. And that type of character, that type of integrity not only brings real fulfillment to our own hearts, but also has a great effect on the lives of all the people around us.

-Radhanath Swami

"

Humility is the cornerstone of leadership.

-John G. Miller

"

Have the humility to learn from those around you.

-John C. Maxwell

"

Humility about how little I know has encouraged me to listen more carefully and more wisely.

-John Templeton

"

If you want the cooperation of humans around you, you must make them feel they are important, and you do that by being genuine and humble.
-Nelson Mandela

"

Vision and persistence will get you to the top of the leadership mountain,
but only humility will keep you there.
-Orrin Woodward

"

If you are humble nothing will touch you either praise or disgrace, because you know what you are.
-Mother Teresa

"

True humility is being able to accept criticisms as graciously as we accept compliments.
-Sabrina Newby

"

A great man is always willing to be little.
-Ralph Waldo Emerson

"

Humility makes great men twice honorable.
-Benjamin Franklin

"

Humility is a great quality of leadership which derives
respect and not just fear or hatred.
-Yousef Munayyer

"

The only wisdom we can hope to acquire is the wisdom
of humility.
-T.S. Eliot

"

Humility is the secret of the wise.
-Ralph Waldo Emerson

"

Humility is always proof of intelligence.
-Claude Vorilhon

"

Ego kills knowledge, as knowledge requires learning, and
learning requires humility.
-Rolsey

"

Humility is the solid foundation of all virtues.
-Confucius

"

Pride is concerned with who is right. Humility is
concerned with what is right.
-Ezra T. Benson

"

Life is long lesson in humility.
-James M. Barrie

"

Humility is not thinking less of yourself, it's thinking of yourself less.
-Rick Warren

"

We learned about gratitude and humility - that so many people had a hand in our success, from the teachers who inspired us to the janitors who kept our school clean…and we were taught to value everyone's contribution and treat everyone with respect.
-Michelle Obama

"

Power is dangerous unless you have humility.
-Richard J. Daley

"

Humility, I have learned, must never be confused with meekness. Humility is being open to the ideas of others.
-Simon Sinek

"

The best leaders are humble enough to realize their victories depend upon their people.
-John C. Maxwell

"

True humility does not know that it is humble. If it did, it would be proud from the contemplation of so fine a virtue.
-Martin Luther

"

If we learn not humility, we learn nothing.
-John Jewel

"

Humility is the key characteristic of a worship leader. Actually, the key for any great leader.
-Chris Tomlin

"

Do you wish to rise? Begin by descending. You plan a
tower that will pierce the clouds?
Lay first the foundation of humility.
-Saint Augustine

"

Humility is simply believing and accepting what God
says about us. And God says that we are anything but
worthless.
-Myles Munroe

"

Humility is a safeguard against humiliation.
-George H. Brimhall

"

So humble yourselves before God. Resist the devil, and
he will flee from you. Come close to God, and God will
come close to you.
-James 4: 7-8

"

When pride comes, then comes disgrace, but with
humility comes wisdom.
-Proverbs 11: 2

"

The higher we are placed, the more humbly we should
walk.
-Unknown

"

We are all stumblers', and the beauty and meaning of life
are in the stumbling.
-David Brooks

"

Humility, like gratitude, is not so much a technique as it
is a way of life.
-Ed Latimore

"

I always say be humble but be firm.
Humility and openness are the key to success without
compromising your beliefs.
-George Hickenlooper

"

If you are not humble, life will visit
humbleness upon you.
-Mike Tyson

"

Avoid having your ego so close to your position that
when your position falls, your ego goes with it.
-Collin Powell

"

If you want to lift yourself up, lift up someone else.
-Booker T. Washington

"

Be kind, work hard, stay humble, smile often, stay loyal, be honest, travel when possible, never stop learning, and love always.
-Unknown

"

Pride makes us artificial and humility makes us real.
-Thomas Merton

"

Pride must die in you, or nothing of heaven can live in you.
-Andrew Murray

"

Selflessness is humility. Humility and freedom go hand in hand. Only a humble person can be free.
-Jeff Wilson

"

Humility isn't denying your strengths; it's being honest about your weaknesses.

-Rick Warren

"

Self-confidence is very important. But without compassion and humility, it's just arrogance.

-Anonymous

"

Being humble means recognizing that we are not on earth to see how important we can become, but to see how much difference we can make in the lives of others.

-Gotdon B. Hincley

"

The ego is your cncmy, not your friend. It is the ego that gives you wounds and hurts you. It is the ego that makes you violent, angry, jealous, and competitive. It is the ego that continuously comparing and feeling miserable.

-Rajneesh

"

Ego is the enemy.
-Ryan Holiday

"

Find a victory in every defeat to remain hopeful and find
a defeat in every victory to remain humble.
-Orrin Woodward

"

Ingratitude produces pride while gratitude produces
humility.
-Orrin Woodward

"

Only humility knows how to appreciate and admire the
good qualities of others.
-Sri Chimmoy

"

What humility does for one is it reminds us that there are people before me, I have already been paid for. And what I need to do is prepare myself so that I can pay for someone else who has yet to come but who may be here and needs me.

-Maya Angelou

"

True leaders don't have ego or pride problems because they know they are here to serve.

-Myles Munroe

ADDITIONAL LEADERSHIP QUOTES

"

Seeds of faith are always within us sometimes it takes a crisis to nourish and encourage their growth.
-Myles Munroe

"

Management is efficiency in climbing the ladder of success; leadership determines whether the ladder is leaning against the right wall.
-Stephen Covey

"

The growth and development of people is the highest calling of leadership.
-John C. Maxwell

"

The best managers and leaders help people become more independent, more capable, and more confident.
-Paul Thornton

"

Corporate culture matters. How management chooses to treat its people impacts everything-for better or for worse.
-Simon Sinek

"

Problems almost create opportunities—to learn, grow, and improve.
-John C. Maxwell

"

Leadership is not about title or designation. It's about impact, influence, and inspiration.
-Robin S. Sharma

"

If you are doing great things, you attract great men. If you are doing little things, you attract little men. Little men usually cause trouble.
-Winston Churchill

"

Unless a man undertakes more than he possibly can do,
he will never do all he can do.
-Henry Drummond

"

Courage is what it takes to stand up and speak; courage is
also what it takes to sit down and listen.
-Richard Branson

"

Actions, not words, are the ultimate results of leadership.
-Bill Owens

"

The secret of leadership is simple: Do what you believe
in. Paint a picture of the future. Go there. People will
follow.
-Seth Godin

"

Good teams are committed to the team mission and to each other personally. Good leaders inspire and build this commitment and trust.

-Lee Ellis

"

Good leaders know who they are their strengths, weaknesses, passions, talents, and values. And, developing leaders always starts with self-awareness.

-Lee Ellis

"

Nobody is going to pour truth into your brain. It's something you have to find out for yourself.

-Noam Chomsky

"

Leadership is for those who love the public good and are endowed and trained to administer it.

-Thornton Wilder

"

A coach is someone who can give correction without
causing resentment.
-John Wooden

"

Twenty years from now you will be more disappointed by
the things that you didn't do than by the ones you did do.
So throw off the bowlines. Sail away from the safe
harbor. Catch the trade winds in your sails. Explore.
Dream. Discover.
-Mark Twain

"

Champions never complain,
they are too busy getting better.
-John Wooden

"

If you are truly a leader, you will help others to not just
see themselves as they are, but also what they can
become.
-David P. Schloss

"

No matter how old you are now. You are never too young
or too old for success or going after what you want.
-Pablo

"

Little values comes out of the belief that people will
respond progressively better by treating them
progressively worse.
-Eric Harvey

"

Your talent and giftedness as a leader have potential to
take you farther than your character can sustain you. That
ought to scare you.
-Andy Stanley

"

Good leadership consists of showing average people how
to do the work of superior people.
-John D. Rockefeller

"

Men are governed only by serving them. The rule is without exception.

-V.cousin

"

Always remember that the future comes one time at a time.

-Dean Acheson

"

Love is the energy of life.

-Robert Browning

"

Success is predictable.

-Brian Tracy

"

Quality is not an act, it is a habit.

-Aristote

"

Instead of reflecting on the past, predict the future.
-Chris Guillebeau

"

Fear is never a reason for quitting; it is only an excuse.
-Norman Vincent Peale

"

You cannot buy or win happiness. You must choose it.
-John C. Maxwell

"

You must remain focused on your journey to greatness.
-Les Brown

"

Winning is not everything, but the effort to win is.
-Zig Ziglar

"

Leadership looks a lot like loving people.
-Unknown

"

Success occurs when your dreams get bigger than your excuses.
-Zig Ziglar

"

There is a difference between working together and working in the same office.
-Simon Sinek

"

It's better to look ahead and prepare, than to look back and regret.
-Jackie Joyner Kensee

"

When we tell people to do their jobs. We get workers. When we trust people to get the job done, we get leaders.
-Simon Sinek

"

A leader's job is to look into the future and see the organization, not as it is, but as it should be.
-Jack Welch

"

The best example of leadership is leadership by example.
-Jerry McClain

"

Trying to manage a project without project management is like trying to play a football game without a game plan.
-Karen Tate

"

Everyone on your team is important…
Importance knows no rank.
-Mike Krzyzewski

"

Champions keep playing until they get it right.
-Billie Jean King

"

Do not let what you cannot do interfere with what you can do.
-John Wooden

"

Do you know what my favorite part of the game is? The opportunity to play.
-Mike Singletary

"

The best teams are made up of a bunch of nobodies who love everybody and serve anybody and don't care about becoming a somebody.
-Phildooley

"

The hard days are the best because that's where champions are made.
-Gabby Douglas

"

It's not the will to win that matters—everyone has that. It's the will to prepare to win that matters.
-Paul Bryant

"

Children are not a distraction from more important work. They are the most important work.
-CS LEWIS

"

Average players want to left alone. Good players want to be coached. Great players want to be told the truth.-Nick Saban

"

It's your response to winning and losing that makes you a winner or a loser.

-Harry Sheeny

"

Bad teams, no one leads. Average teams, coaches lead. But elite teams, players lead.

-PJ F

"

The culture precedes positive results. It doesn't get tacked on as an afterthought on your way to the victory stand. Champions behave like champions before they're champions: they have a winning standard of performance before they are winners.

-Bill Walsh

"

When you were made a leader, you weren't given a grown; you were given the responsibility to bring out the best in others.
-Jack Welch

"

Your greatest asset should be your work ethic.
-Kevin Garnett

"

Added pressure and responsibility should not change one's leadership style, it should merely expose that which already exists.
-Mark W. Boyer

"

Leadership is working with goals and vision; management is working with objectives.
-Russel Honore

"

Managers think of the next position, leaders think of the next generation.
-Myles Munroe

"

What great leaders have in common is that each truly knows his or her strengths-and can call on the right strength at the right time.
-Tom Rath

"

Leadership is just another word for training.
-Lance Secretan

"

The single biggest way to impact an organization is to focus on leadership development. There is almost no limit to the potential of an organization that recruits good people, raises them up as leaders and continually develops them.
-John C. Maxwell

"

Leaders instill in their people a hope for success and a belief in themselves. Positive leaders empower people to accomplish their goals.

-Unknown

"

Leading is influencing, guiding in direction, course, action, opinion.

-Warren Bennis

"

Leverage is the ability to apply positive pressure on yourself to follow through on your decisions even when it hurts.

-Orrin Woodward

"

Taking charge of your own learning is a part of taking charge of your life, which is the sine qua non in becoming an integrated person.

-Warren G. Bennis

"

Leadership - mobilization toward a common goal.
-Gary Wills

"

Do not follow where the path may lead. Go instead where
no path is and leave a trail.
-Muriel Strode

"

Everyone carries a bucket of water and a bucket of gas in
life. A leader has learned to throw the right one at the
right time.
-Orrin Woodward

"

Leading is influencing, guiding in direction, course,
action, opinion.
-Warren Bennis

"

Leverage is the ability to apply positive pressure on yourself to follow through on your decisions even when it hurts.
-Orrin Woodward

"

Taking charge of your own learning is a part of taking charge of your life, which is the sine qua non in becoming an integrated person.
-Warren G. Bennis

"

The role of the leader is not to come up with all the great ideas. The role of a leader is to create an environment in which great ideas can happen.
-Simon Sinek

"

Leaders who don't listen will eventually be surrounded by people who have nothing to say.
-Andy Stanley

"

Leaders don't seek followers.
Followers are attracted to leaders.
-Myles Munroe

"

The role of the leader is not to come up with all the great
ideas. The role of a leader is to create an environment in
which great ideas can happen.
-Simon Sine

"

If you fail, don't be too sad. If you succeed, don't be too
proud. Just keep learning and keep trying.
-Jack Ma

"

Personality is how you respond on a typical day.
Character is how you show up on your worst day.
-Adam Grant

CONCLUSION

Thank you for Investing your precious time in exploring this compilation. May you discover not just information, but profound inspiration that fuels your journey towards becoming the very best version of yourself. Remember, as you navigate the path of leadership, this document can serve as a compass, a constant source of education, and a wellspring of wisdom.

Leadership transcends mere positions; it's a disposition, a state of being. Regardless of where you currently stand in your leadership role – be it as a parent, teacher, pastor, manager, CEO, or entrepreneur – let the essence of your leadership emanate from within. Consistency in your commitment to personal growth is the key; for, as you already know, 'Growth is not an automatic process.' It requires deliberate intention and focused effort to cultivate the leader within you.

I extend my heartfelt wishes for nothing but the absolute best on your leadership journey. May you find the strength to persevere, the courage to innovate, and the wisdom to lead with compassion. Keep growing, keep leading the way, and may your impact resonate in every role you embrace. The world awaits the extraordinary leader within you. Embrace the journey, and may it be nothing short of remarkable.

BILIOGRAPHY

- John C. Maxwell. "Developing the Leader within You," April 1993
- John C. Maxwell. Developing the Leader around You, February 22, 1995
- Stephen R. Covey. "The 7 Habits of Highly Effective" People, August 15, 1989
- Joey Jenkins. "Never Hit The Snooze Button," June 15, 2018
- Jocko Willink. "Extreme Ownership," October 20, 2015
- Myles Munroe. "The principles and Power of Vision," June 1, 2003
- Myles Munroe. "The Power of Character in Leadership," June 2013
- Goal cast. (http://www.goalcast.com)
- Inc magazine. (http://www.inc.com)
- Forbes magazine. (http://www.forbes.com)
- Goodreads. (http://www.goodreads.com)
- BrainyQuote. (http://www.brainyquote.com)

About the Author

Belisier Chery is a dedicated blogger, entrepreneur, and visionary leader. He is the founder and CEO of BC BUSINESS GROUP, a company with a global mission to empower and guide young entrepreneurs in adopting a transformative leadership mindset for creating sustainable, long-term impacts. A passionate advocate for change, Belisier is also the co-founder of Clickmart, a platform designed to connect students across Haiti, inspiring them with insights into entrepreneurship and leadership.

Drawing from his upbringing as a farmer working alongside his father in raising goats and cows, Belisier understands the essence of sustainable agribusinesses in driving a nation's economic growth. With a strong commitment to his homeland, he has embarked on a mission to establish viable agribusiness ventures in Haiti that will contribute significantly to the country's economy.

Beyond his entrepreneurial pursuits, Belisier has consistently demonstrated a deep sense of community and compassion. His years of experience serving as a Sunday school teacher and mentoring children by imparting computer skills in an orphanage highlight his dedication to nurturing growth and fostering the best in people.

Belisier is currently pursuing a degree in business management, aiming to enhance his knowledge and skills to further his mission of building sustainable businesses that will elevate Haiti's economic landscape.

To connect with Belisier Chery, you can reach out to him via email at belisierchery@gmail.com and you can stay updated with his inspiring work and insights by following him on social media.